v

Wheatgrass:

Growing and Juicing for Better Nutrition

by Julia Winchester

Published by Cardigan River LLC

Copyright © Julia Winchester 2012

Disclaimer

Table of Contents

Chapter 1: An Introduction to Wheatgrass

Perhaps you've noticed the presence of wheatgrass in health food stores or at health bars. If you haven't given it a try because you were not sure what it is, make sure you sample it next time. Often referred to as a tool for rejuvenating the body, this substance is becoming more popular than ever. One of the reasons it's so great is because it is good for you.

You'll see it used in various ways including:

- Smoothies

- Additions to salads

- As a fresh juice ingredient

- Taken as a tablet

- Consumed as a powder

The fact is that this very nutritious food is versatile. It is not new, either. In fact, many professional athletes have used it for years to improve their ability to remain healthy. As a dry product, it has been sold regularly to the general public for quite some time. It may be time for you to try it, too.

Who Should Be Reading This?

There is no one that shouldn't learn about the health benefits and the good-for-you qualities of wheatgrass. In fact, if you are like most people, you need this. Do you eat fast food on a regular basis? Do you find yourself pushing those greens to the side of your plate at each meal?

Perhaps you do wish you could eat a more health-based diet but think it's too hard to do so.

Even if you are eating a healthy diet for the most part, chances are high of you not getting enough of the nutrition you need. The American diet, for example, is packed with fat. Soils are often depleted of nutrients and that means the food you consume is also lacking in the nutrition you need. This is one of the reasons why eating organic food is so valuable. It can provide you with the best possible quality of nutrients in what you are consuming. Organic wheatgrass is a critical staple for supplementing any diet.

It's Not a Gimmick and It's Not Expensive

One of the two biggest worries many people have today about the health food they buy is whether or not they are just buying a gimmick, or a food with a promised level of nutrition that never fully occurs. That's really not what wheatgrass is. In fact, you could eat a huge box of green vegetables and not get the same nutrition you would get from a serving of wheatgrass in some situations.

Then there's the concern that it is too expensive. Many foods that are healthier for you tend to have a higher price point. That's shocking since it is often what people need the most to feel well and to have the energy they need. The good news is that wheatgrass does not cost a lot of money. In fact, we will tell you how to grow your own if you would like to do so.

Inexpensive, packed with nutrition, even something you can grow in your backyard, wheatgrass is necessary for many people's diets. Are you ready to learn what it is?

So, What Is Wheatgrass Then?

The Mayo Clinic provides some good information about what wheatgrass is and why it should be a part of your diet. First, let's talk about what this nutrient-rich food is.

This is a type of young grass. It is in the wheat family. Some have called it the king of all grains. It comes from the Red Wheat Berry. This very specific type of berry is important because it produces this grain that is very high in active enzymes, vitamins, antioxidants, chlorophyll and vital amino acids. No other berry is a good substitution for this one.

When it is growing, wheat grass is a green plant that's lush. As it grows, it becomes more of a shaft, much like you would see in any other form of grass. It then grows small grains at the top, which can be harvested.

However, in the grass stage, it is significantly different. That happens long before the grain is harvested. At about seven days, the wheat grass has grown to about six to nine inches in length. At this point, it is cut (before it goes to grain production). It can then be dried thoroughly and used as a powder.

In other words, it is like the nutrients that come from an egg. Eggs are highly rich in nutrition and good fats. That's not necessarily the same nutrients present in the chicken, though. Rather, these high levels of nutrition found in the egg are meant to give the chicken a real chance at developing into a healthy creature. The same is true for wheatgrass.

Because wheatgrass is so densely packed with nutrition, which is nature's intent to give the plant the ability to grow to the point of creating grains or seeds, by cutting it at this early stage, we are accessing all of those amazing nutrients that are locked within it. We are able to get all of the nutrition from it, including the enzymes, minerals, vitamins, and chlorophyll meant to help the plant to grow.

In this book, we will discuss the numerous types of health benefits that wheatgrass can bring to you, but don't look at it as a solution to your health problems. In other words, you do not have to have these health problems to use wheatgrass. Anyone of any background can benefit from it.

If you are new to it, don't push it aside as something you don't have to eat. Don't assume it is the same as wheat either. Rather, focus on the true quality of nutrition that stems from this one source.

Chapter 2: The Health Benefits of Wheatgrass

Anyone who is looking for a way to improve their health, raise their energy levels or overcome various ailments needs to improve their diet. What we know is that the body's immune systems, hormone balances and organ function all relate to the quality, not the quantity, of food we eat. By boosting the health qualities of the foods we consume, we can drastically see an improvement in the body's natural ability to heal itself and to manage stresses.

Wheatgrass can give you much of the nutrition you need. Some very important components to its makeup make it a must-have in any diet. Specifically, consider the benefits of chlorophyll, antioxidants, the vitamins and the amino acids found within it.

What's in Wheatgrass?

Look at the following list of nutrients found in wheatgrass, as the Mayo Clinic notes. You'll find it is packed with the nutrition you know you need.

- Iron

- Calcium

- Magnesium

- Vitamins A, C and E

- Chlorophyll

All of these vitamins are important to your overall health and function. They help control many of the activities in your body. Let's break down the most important components included in wheatgrass further.

The Benefits and Power of Chlorophyll

When it comes to wheatgrass, one of the main nutrients you will hear a great deal about is chlorophyll. What is it?

This is a specific type of protein found only in plant composition. It is similar to the human red blood cells. It has various benefits to the human body including:

- It improves gastrointestinal problems. Because it is able to flush out the colon, it can help release some of the triggers for various diseases in this area. It improves digestion, too.

- It works to promote red blood cell and hemoglobin production in the body. Seventy-five percent of your blood is composed of hemoglobin. This iron-rich substance is critical to the transportation of oxygen throughout the body's tissues, cells, and organs. In other words, when you consume this nutrient, you are getting a significant increase in the energy flowing through your body.

- It is an ideal tool for detoxing. If you want to remove some or all of the toxins that cause cancer from your body, this solution can do that. Carcinogen substances are prevented when you consume chlorophyll. A derivative of this substance, called chlorophyllin, helps to latch onto carcinogens in your body, and removes them from the body.

- It can help your body to use heavy minerals as well as calcium properly. It is able to enter into the blood stream faster than most other foods. It then assimilates calcium and other nutrients so that your tissues can be rebuilt and replaced at a faster pace.

- It can treat bad breath, too. It works as a deodorizer in this way by ridding the source of the problem.

- It can help to fight infections. Because it is an antioxidant, it will naturally help to fight off any inflammation occurring in the body.

5

As you can see, this one nutrient that makes up wheatgrass is vitally important to the health and well-being of your body. And, that's just one component of it!

The Antioxidants in Wheatgrass

You know the value of antioxidants in your diet. Antioxidants are the powerhouses when it comes to cleaning out your body and removing toxins. Imagine these small little nutrients racing through your bloodstream. They come across plaque buildup in your arteries and help to push it off, giving you clearer arteries. They work to flush out toxins from cells, which can help to refresh the way you look and even help to boost your energy levels.

Antioxidants are a critical component to overcoming and preventing diseases of all types. The more antioxidants you eat every day, the better you look, and feel, not to mention the better your health is.

Wheatgrass contains a large number of important antioxidants. You'll find that the antioxidants in wheatgrass may help with:

- Improving arthritis

- Fighting off cancer

- Reducing premature aging

- Getting rid of cataracts

- Managing nervous disorders

- Avoiding or repairing of arterial damage

While no one is saying it is a cure, these antioxidants will work very hard at helping to improve your body's health. Their goal is to find and get rid of free radicals in your body. Free radicals are the toxins stored throughout it that are causing your inflammation and disease.

These antioxidants in wheatgrass have some astonishing benefits. In one study, conducted in 2006 by a group of Indian scientists, there was clear evidence that the antioxidants in wheatgrass were not only present but were at a very high level. What they found was that wheatgrass has a higher level of antioxidants than most other vegetables.

The Vitamins in Wheatgrass

Next, let's take a closer look at the vitamins found in wheatgrass and why they matter. Remember, some of these vitamins are the antioxidants we mentioned previously. Here are some of the vitamins found in wheatgrass and their importance to your diet.

Vitamin A

One of the most important vitamins found in wheatgrass is Vitamin A. Wheatgrass provides twice the amount of vitamin A, in fact, than a serving of carrots. This nutrient is very important for maintaining vision. It is an antioxidant. It works to keep your skin healthy and fight off infections and some types of diseases.

Vitamin C

Another nutrient found in high amounts in wheatgrass is Vitamin C. Most commonly found in fruits such as kiwi, lemons, and oranges, there is a significant amount of it in wheatgrass. Wheatgrass has more Vitamin C, in fact, than a serving of oranges. This nutrient is critical to your health. It helps you to develop a strong immune system able of fighting off infection. Additionally, it can help in fighting allergies and asthma while also working as prevention against cardiovascular disease.

B Vitamins

The B vitamins contained within wheatgrass include B1, B2, B3, B5, B6, B8 and B12. The last one is perhaps the most well-known by most people because it is a great source of energy. B vitamins offer various benefits to your health. They can help prevent heart disease and cancer. They work to help maintain healthy skin and hair. They work to maintain muscle tone throughout your body. They even boost metabolism.

Vitamin K

Vitamin K is not as well known as others, but it is still very important to your health. It is found in wheatgrass. It can help with reducing cancer risks, preventing the onset or worsening of osteoporosis, managing clot formation in the body and even helping to minimize menstrual pain.

The Amino Acids in Wheatgrass

Next, let's take a look at the amino acids found in wheatgrass. What are they? These organic compounds are a type of building block within your body specifically related to proteins. They are often produced in the body, but there are 10 of them that are called essential amino acids. These cannot be produced by your body but must come to you in the form of your food. That's where wheatgrass comes in to help out.

As the building block of protein, amino acids are necessary in your diet. They work to use proteins and enzymes. This helps with the development, then the growth and the overall maintenance of every cell in your body.

Some of these include isoleucine, lysine, threonine, and tryptophan. All of the essential amino acids you need are found in wheatgrass. For example, studies indicate you need about 20 milligrams of isoleucine in your diet. Wheatgrass has 31 milligrams in it. Leucine, which you should consume about 39 milligrams daily, is available at 57 milligrams in wheatgrass. This is true of nearly all of the essential amino acids found in wheatgrass.

What it all Means

This heavily nutrient-packed food is necessary in your diet. It gives your body many of the nutrients it needs to maintain health, prevent the onset of illness, and fight any conditions already present in your body. Is it a cure? Not necessarily. However, it is a nutrient-rich food that far exceeds the nutrient levels in most of the foods people are consuming today.

Chapter 3: The Supplies for Growing and Juicing Wheatgrass

Now that you know the health benefits of this nutrient-rich food, you probably want to have it within your diet. Let's focus specifically on the supplies you'll need in this chapter.

Before we do that, though, it's important to know why you should take the time to grow it. You can, of course, go to your health food store and buy some of the product directly. That will work, but you may not get the actual healthiest source. In other words, if you want the ground up product with no effort at all, do buy it. However, if you want to have more nutrition and the very best quality, it's best to grow it from home.

There's some good news, though. It is easy to grow it at home. You'll learn how to do that in the next chapter. However, you do not need a lot of space and no plowing of fields is required here! Rather, you will be able to grow wheatgrass in your home, not even outside if you don't want to, and you'll be able to harvest and consume it when and how you want to. This is the ideal option for those wanting to use wheatgrass in juicing, one of the best possible ways to get the nutrition from it.

The Right Place to Grow

You can grow wheatgrass in virtually any form. The best option, though, is to grow it in a growing tray. You can easily find these online or at your local gardening shop. People use them for all types of indoor growing or sprouting of plants that they plan to transplant outdoors.

You can use a flowerpot or other types of containers as well. No matter what type you select, there are a few things to keep in mind.

- Ensure they are stable enough to hold at least a few inches of soil. They also should be able to be moved if you decide you need to do so at some time.

- If you do not have a lot of room to dedicate to growing wheatgrass in one location, try using smaller pots placed throughout the home instead.

- Be sure there are drainage holes at the bottom of any container or tray you use. You need water to be able to escape so that the seeds and plants themselves are not sitting in water.

Here are some helpful measurements to keep in mind if you are unsure how much you should plan to grow:

- To produce about 10 ounces (0.3 liters) of juice, you'll need about half a pound (225g) of seed or about one cup (1/4 liter) of it. For this amount, you will need a tray that's smaller, about 10 inches by 10 inches (25cm by 25cm) is ideal.

- If you want to produce up to two cups (1/2 liter) of product, or 20 ounces (0.6 liters) of juice, you will need two cups (1/2 liter) or one pound (450g) of seed. However, you can usually use the 17 inches by 17 inches (43cm by 43cm) trays for this without a problem.

If you are unsure if this is something you want to commit a lot of space to, it is a good idea to select a smaller number of seeds to start with and then work your way up as you begin to use them and enjoy them.

Products and Soils

Though some people do grow these hydroponically, that's not necessarily the best option. You want these plants to be able to get the nutrients from the soil you'll use. It is best to use only organic soils. Be sure to look for soils that are nutrient-rich but 100 percent organic. You don't want to put all of the hard work you are doing at risk because the soil you use is full of chemicals and toxins.

You don't have to buy the most expensive product. It will grow well in nearly all types of soils. You can use various forms of soil, including top soil, potting mixtures etc. Be very careful about using organic compost, though. It tends to have a high level of acid in it, which means it will be harder to grow in especially for these seeds.

Strive for Organic, Non-GMO Sources

You will also need to consider the importance of purchasing quality products for both soils and seeds. It is ideal to purchase organics. It is also essential to purchase non-GMO sources. Genetically modified products pose a risk to anyone. The fact is, there is no way to know what role these modified foods are going to play in the next decade or so. They are not natural and, therefore, they should not be a part of this growing process.

The fact is, you are trying to do something good for your body by consuming wheatgrass. Don't ruin it all by consuming a great deal of GMO foods. In other words, seek out non-GMO products whenever possible for this process because it makes sense to do so.

What Else You Will Need

You'll need to purchase the right seeds for wheatgrass. There are varieties of suppliers you can buy from. It is a good idea to get to know the company before you invest significantly. There are some suppliers listed at the back of this book for you to consider. You will find a variety of seed options. This is a plant with many variations. Look for winter wheat seeds, though. They are harvested at a different time of year and are a better quality product.

Additionally, you will need a juicer. We will talk about the specific types of juicers ideal for this. However, plan to invest in a quality product.

Then, you'll need some time and sunlight. It is a good idea to have an open area where you can place the trays where they will get sunlight at least some of the day, during the very start of the growing process. Then, you'll need to move them to an area out of direct sunlight. You want them to have the resources to grow not just quickly but also heartily so you are getting your time and money's worth.

Keep in mind you can reuse most of your supplies with each growth process you follow. It is also a good idea for you to grow in batches, starting each one about a week or more apart from the next one. This way, you have a constant supply of product ready to use whenever you want to do so.

Chapter 4: How to Grow Wheatgrass

Now that you know what goes into the process of growing wheatgrass, you can start the process. The good news is this process is very easy. You do not need any previous gardening experience. You don't even need to know much about the growing process. These plants are very easy to work with for the most part.

Steps to Growing Wheatgrass

With seeds in hand and all of your supplies ready, let's work through some simple steps for planting and growing wheatgrass.

Because these are hard, winter wheat seeds, you do need to get them to open up. To do this, you will want to soak them. Soak them for about eight hours or overnight in warm water.

Place them into a jar. Cover them with water for about 24 hours after this. During this timeframe, rinse them three times.

While this is happening, prepare the soil. Look for an overall good blend. If you need to add peat moss to the mixture, aim for one part peat moss to three parts of the soil itself. Otherwise, use a potting mix. Then, place this into the trays you've purchased. You'll want to add enough soil to be about halfway up the sizes of the tray.

You will notice that a very short tail is forming at this point. That's the good news. That means the seeds are ready to grow. At this point, you can plant them in the soil mixture.

Place the seeds on top of the soil and then push them in just slightly. You do not want them to be buried. Rather, you want that tail to be able to sprout through the soil. Cover them lightly with soil.

Keep the soil wet. You'll want to water it right after planting to saturate it. Do not use a strong stream of water. That will ultimately cause the seeds to wash away. Place the tray's cover on them.

You'll want to use a spray bottle, if possible, to mist the plants every day. Try to gently do this at the same time each day to keep the soil moist. Do this for the first three days.

By the fourth day (sometimes it may take another day or so), you'll see the wheatgrass coming in. You'll want to keep the tray uncovered at this time. Keep it out of direct sunlight. Rather, keep it in a room where there is enough light to see without any artificial light, but not in direct sunlight.

You can grow wheatgrass during the colder months - remember, inside your home, you control the temperature. If you do this, you will need to ensure there is enough light in the space to allow for growth. You also need to ensure that the temperature remains constant. Don't let the temperature dip below 60 degrees Fahrenheit (15 degrees Celsius).

Next, use a fan or some type of ventilation in the room. If it is warm enough, keep a window open. If it is too cold for this, a fan will work. This air circulation is essential for minimizing the risk of mold growth. You also don't want temperatures to go above 80 degrees Fahrenheit (26 degrees Celsius), if possible. This also can be a contributing factor to mold growth in these plants.

Give the process time. You may need to adjust the amount of sunlight or the amount of moisture you are providing to encourage the plants to grow. However, this plant likes to grow quickly so you will see results right away.

Harvesting Your Wheatgrass

As you watch your wheatgrass grow, you'll be amazed at just how fast the process is. You may find that you want to try it sooner rather than later. However, the timing of cutting and using it is very simplistic to manage.

Remember, you do not want to allow it to grow too long otherwise it will become a hollowed stalk with grains at the top of it. At that point, the nutrients in the plant are gone. You need to harvest it well before that.

As it grows, you will notice that it splits. This happens when a second blade of grass will appear at the bottom of the current blade. If you see that happen, you know that the process is ready. Generally, this process takes between a week and 12 days. Various factors will affect how fast it occurs, including the climate of the home and the seeds themselves. However, you do not want to make your harvesting based on the size of the plant but rather the sprouting of the secondary blade.

You do not want to cut too late. It is better to cut it too soon rather than wait too long. As it gets taller, it will become bitterer and that makes it less healthy and less good tasting!

Once you are ready to harvest it, all you need is a pair of sharp scissors. Wash and dry them so they are clean enough for the process. Then, cut the wheatgrass just above the level of the soil. The lower you cut the better. Cut all of the grass from this production at one time. You do not want to come back and trim off just what you need since this means that the wheatgrass will continue to grow.

Once you cut it, you can rinse it off under cool water. Then, dry it, wrap it in a clean, dry paper towel and store in a sealed plastic bag until you are ready to use it. Generally, you can store it like this for up to a week or two. There are also "green bags" which are designed to keep vegetables healthy and fresh longer. You can use these as well. Be sure to store them in a cold portion of the refrigerator at about 38 degrees Fahrenheit (3 degrees Celsius).

Now what?

Now that you've cut the wheatgrass and are storing it, the next step is to start over. You will notice that a second sprouting is likely to occur with these plants. However, they will lack most of the nutrition you want. The first harvest is the very best. It is a good idea, then, to start over with new seeds.

It is a smart idea to start a new seed tray every five to seven days. That way, once you get into a rhythm, you will have a regular harvest of wheatgrass every week. This, of course, depends on how much you would like to have and how often you will need it.

Chapter 5: Juicing and Wheatgrass Go Hand in Hand

Juicing is the ideal way to enjoy wheatgrass. Not only does it provide you with ample nutrition, but it is easy to blend with other fruits and vegetables, though many people prefer it alone.

Juicing is the process of taking the fresh wheatgrass you've just harvested and using a specialized blender, fitted as a juicer, to do the work for you. It will liquefy the wheatgrass so you can drink it and therefore, bring in all of the nutrition.

Why is juicing so important?

In order to get to the nutrients found in wheatgrass or any type of plant, it is essential to break down the cell walls. That means that if you chew it, you are only getting a small amount of the nutrition out. However, when you juice it, all of those nutrients are fast flowing right from the wheatgrass itself into your body's digestion system and cells. By juicing, you get the nutrition more thoroughly and faster than if you were to try and just eat it as is.

Specialized Juicers Are a Must

You should not use just any blender for juicing wheatgrass. Instead of a blender or a food processor, select a juicer designed for wheatgrass or products like it. Blenders and any type of food processor work very quickly. As a blender spins rapidly, it is definitely pulverizing the plant, but it is also oxidizing the chlorophyll within it. This fast movement is not good for the protection of this important nutrient.

Instead, you need a juicer. You can even use a mortar and pestle if you want to keep it very basic. However, that's not recommended as you'll need to have a strong forearm muscle to drain enough juice out of it. Rather, check for a juicer designed for the wheatgrass itself.

You will find wheatgrass juicers sold just like this. Several manufacturers offer them. These juicers are designed to extract the juice from most types of leafy greens, which means it is a versatile enough machine to invest in. However, you do not want to use these juicers for most fruits or vegetables. You need a separate one for wheatgrass.

Single or Doubles?

You can find single wheatgrass juicers or you can purchase a double. Double varieties are designed to work for wheatgrass on one side. On the other side, a separate juicer is available to do your fruits and vegetables. These are ideal if you are planning to do a great deal of juicing or you want to be able to mix these.

Manual Wheatgrass Juicers

The most common form of juicer for wheatgrass is a manual variety. Yes, you will need to crank these over and over again to get them to extract the juice from the plant. That's a good thing. They will pull out the nutrients you need and give it to you in a juice form without destroying the nutrients within.

If you are buying a manual juicer, consider the following:

- Be sure it is easy to clean.

- Most are compact and easy to store even in an apartment or a small kitchen.

- Look for those that have a suction clamp or base clamp. These hold the juicer in place as you rotate the handle. Otherwise, it would move around and make the process difficult.

- It should have a stainless steel grinding plate. This ensures it is going to be efficient while also ensuring it is easy to maintain.

- You'll want to ensure it is not made with any toxic polycarbonate products.

- Most will have some basic features and accessories. You'll want those that have a plunger, to push the wheatgrass into the opening so you don't lose a finger.

- Most will have a year or more warranty. That's a good thing.

Motorized Juicers

There are also those varieties of wheatgrass juicers designed with a motor on them. Let's say you don't have much time or arm strength to handle the manual varieties. That's okay. These do work very well if you buy a specialized wheatgrass variety. There are a few things to look for.

- Be sure the feed chute is large enough. Those that are at least 1.5 inches are ideal.

- You want to be sure it is lightweight. Some models can become very heavy and hard to manage.

- Look for at least 220 watts of power from the motor. This will give you enough power to get through the juice at the right speed.

- It should also have a warranty of at least a year.

- It should also have a screen and auger for use.

Overall, any of these juicers are going to be a good option if they are designed specifically for wheatgrass. Compare models closely. You don't necessarily have to choose the most expensive variety.

The Process of Juicing Wheatgrass

Now that you have your juicer, you'll want to start blending away. This is a very simple process.

Remember the following measurements:

- To get about 10 ounces (0.3 liters) of wheatgrass juice, you'll need a tray that is about 10 inches by 10 inches (25cm by 25cm).

- For 20 ounces (0.6 liters) of juice, you'll need a tray that is about 17 inches by 17 inches (43cm by 43cm).

This can vary significantly depending on how many seeds you added and how well they did.

To juice them, harvest them as described earlier. Then, cut them in half to make handling and processing them easy. Add some to the juicer, following the instructions from your specific juicer manufacturer on how to use the device properly. You are going to need to add a bit of water to the process to create a paste.

That's all it takes. You can then take this liquid and mix it in with whatever smoothie or other recipe you would like. There's nothing more to it!

Storing Wheatgrass Juice

Once you have your wheatgrass juice created, there's more good news. You can actually store it for between 24 and 48 hours in an airtight container in the refrigerator. During that time, you can drink it or add it to your smoothies. This means you should process your wheatgrass in the morning or in the evening and then have it for the next day.

Use a pitcher to make pouring easy. Just ensure the container of wheatgrass has a lid on at all times because it can pick up the flavors from the refrigerator otherwise. You also want to shake it well prior to using in order to redistribute the particles evenly into the water.

Chapter 6: Composting the Waste from Growing and Juicing

Now that you've started to grow your own wheatgrass and make juice, you will notice you will have some leftovers after the process is over. This includes the remaining seeds and roots, as well as some of the thick paste from the juicing process. It is a very good idea to use these nutrient-rich foods.

If you want to be truly organic and environmentally friendly, change your thinking on how you grow wheatgrass. You can use biodegradable mats in an effort to make this process even better for the earth.

Keep the following in mind if you consider going this route:

- You can find biodegradable mats available online through farm supplies or through specialized retailers. The goal is to use them and then toss them into the compost.

- You can use soil more than one time to grow your wheatgrass. As long as you remove the matted roots of the system, you can easily reuse any loose soil in a new tray for a new set of seeds.

Another way many people make this process biodegradable is to simply use all the mats created from the growing process of wheatgrass as compost. After you harvest the plants, the soil and roots remaining will form a very dense mat. This is all nutrient-rich. While you don't want to eat dirt, you can add it to your compost heap and allow it to become a rich soil additive to gardens later on.

This method allows you to benefit from not wasting a single thing. No matter if you buy a specially designed mat for this or you just compost the current mat you have created from the soil and root mixture, don't let this go to waste.

Tips for Creating Compost

To create a barrel of compost that's great for your garden or for other uses, follow these specific steps. It is super easy to do this using even a trashcan you may have.

Using a barrel you've purchased and washed clean, drill holes about two inches (5cm) apart across the diameter of the barrel to allow for air circulation.

Add the wheatgrass mats to the compost barrel as you create them. Break them into pieces for better breakdown.

Add in all of your wheatgrass paste or other compost from the juicer you may have.

You can also add in all of the vegetable scraps you have in the home. Keep it all-organic and be sure that you do not add meat-based products or processed foods to the mix.

Add in earthworms that will do the work for you. They will take care of breaking down the material for you. Cover the barrel with a lid during this time.

You can continue to add to this over time. Try to add a wheatgrass mat in between layers of food scraps, though. You should not need to add any additional earthworms.

Mix it weekly after a month. In about two months, you'll have rich soil to use.

Composting just makes sense as you continue to develop your organic lifestyle.

Chapter 7: Additional Uses and Recipes for Wheatgrass

Using wheatgrass is easy to do. As stated earlier, you can easily take the actual sprouts and add them to your salads. You can add them into virtually any smoothie that you already make and enjoy for added nutrition. To help you to enjoy it, here are some great recipes to use when enjoying wheatgrass.

In these recipes, you'll see the approximate amount of wheatgrass to use listed as a size. That's how much wheatgrass prior to juicing you will need. It is still preferred to juice wheatgrass separately and then add it into the blender or mixer with the other nutrients for optimal health.

"Keep It Simple" Green Smoothie

Here is a great option for those who want a simple, good-for-you solution for energy and vitality.

- Use about a two to three-inch (5cm to 7.5cm) round of wheatgrass

- Two stalks of celery

- 1 cup (1/4 liter) of spinach leaves

- 1/2 cup (1/8 liter) of parsley

- 1/3 cup (80ml) of water

Blend well and enjoy like this or over ice for a cool treat.

Simple Wheatgrass Smoothie

This option has some tang to it. You will enjoy it for breakfast or anytime.

- 3-inch (7.5cm) round of wheatgrass

- 2 oranges juiced

- 1 banana

- 1 lime juiced

- 2 cups (1/2 liter) of ice, crushed

Blend the juices together and then add in the ice. It has an invigorating quality to it that is incredibly unique and delicious tasting.

Carrot and Wheatgrass Mixture

Carrots go well with wheatgrass. For a very simple smoothie, simply juice three carrots and add a 3-inch round (7.5cm) of wheatgrass to it. You can add some water to liquefy it more so than it is. It is very good for you and very effective at stimulating the metabolism. It takes just a few seconds to make, too.

Vegetable Wheatgrass Smoothie

Many of the best recipes for wheatgrass include fruit, but that's to taste. You can create smoothies using just vegetables, too. They make a fantastic treat you'll enjoy as a meal replacement.

- 2 carrots

- 4 inches (10cm) of wheatgrass

- 3 large stalks of celery

- 1/2 cup (1/8 liter) fresh parsley

- 1/2 of a beet root

- 2 cup (1/2 liter) of fresh spinach leaves

- 1/2 cup (1/8 liter) of alfalfa sprouts or other sprouts you enjoy

This one is a fantastic option because it gives you a sense of being full and produces a good amount of juice for you to enjoy. Be sure to mix in your favorite vegetables with this. You can tailor it to your tastes or whatever you have available in the refrigerator.

Energy Shake with Wheatgrass

If you need a boost in the morning or want more energy in the middle of the day, this wheatgrass based energy shake works very well. It may become your favorite choice.

- 1 cup (1/4 liter) of crushed pineapple

- 1 banana

- 1 cup (1/4 liter) of apple

- 2 inch (5cm) round of wheatgrass

Mix it together and add it to your favorite shaker. You can then take it to work with you whenever you want to do so. Enjoy it in the middle of the day if you like, but keep it in the refrigerator in the meantime.

Vinaigrette with Wheatgrass

Another way to use wheatgrass juice is in the form of a dressing for your favorite salad. That's a fantastic way to get even more nutrition into your family and the kids will never even know! Here's a simple recipe for doing this, but you can add about one to two inches (2.5 to 5cm) of wheatgrass to your favorite vinaigrette to create your own version, too.

- 1 cup (1/4 liter) of extra virgin olive oil

- 1 cup (1/4 liter) of rice wine vinegar (or your favorite type)

- 1 chopped clove of garlic

- 3-inches (7.5cm) of wheatgrass juiced

- 1 teaspoon (5ml) of cayenne pepper if you want some heat with it

- 1/2 teaspoon (2.5ml) of black pepper or crushed red pepper flakes

- 1/2 teaspoon (2.5ml) of salt to taste

Mix all of this in a container with a lid to blend well. You can also add it to a blender. Store it in an airtight container in the refrigerator for up to a week to use, as you need to. Be sure to play with those spices and ingredients to create your own favorites. The longer they sit together prior to being enjoyed, the more blended the flavors will be.

In an Ice Cream?

Do you have an ice cream maker at home? How about a sorbet maker? If so, you can add the juiced wheatgrass to the mixture you are creating of your favorite flavors and have a very healthy option. A good option, for example, is any fruit-flavored organic sorbet and a mixture of just 1-inch (2.5cm) of wheatgrass that's been juiced.

Now, to make this even simpler, if you do not have your own machine, do this. Allow the sorbet or your other favorite treat to melt slightly. Place the serving you would like into a blender and then add the juiced wheatgrass to the mixture. Then, place into a plastic container with a lid and put in the freezer for about an hour. This will create a brand new flavor that has the wheatgrass mixed in with it.

What Else Can You Do With It?

You can make the juice from the wheatgrass and add it into virtually any type of meal you are creating. This includes both cold and cooked foods. Here are a few more ideas for you:

- Add it into potato salads or macaroni salads for a tangy addition

- Add it into soups. Again, the kids will not even know it is there.

- Add it into your favorite alcoholic beverage for a tempting and almost good-for-you treat (alcoholic or not!)

- Add it to weight loss shakes or other dietary aids you are taking to increase your energy levels and improve your health without many calories.

- Add it into stews or other cooked meals.

As you can see, this is a very versatile ingredient that you can use in virtually any way that you would like. It can be beneficial, though, just to have a few drinks of it straight from the juicer. You can sweeten it with a bit of honey or add some heat to it with a dash of cayenne. Depending on your mood, you can really make this into something that you enjoy.

Chapter 8: Additional Resources

There are many outstanding reasons to enjoy wheatgrass. Of course, it does taste good. If you are ready to start enjoying it, be sure to consider the following resources. These, which were used in this book as well as for further research, can help you get the most out of this healthy plant that you never knew was such a great option.

For additional reading material, please visit:

- http://www.alliancegym.com/6-chlorophyll-benefits-healing-powers/

- http://onlinelibrary.wiley.com/doi/10.1002/ptr.1838/abstract

- http://www.livestrong.com/article/285913-vitamins-in-wheatgrass/

- http://healthyeating.sfgate.com/amount-amino-acids-wheat-grass-1211.html

- http://drwheatgrass.com/ - This site has a great deal of information about the overall health benefits of wheatgrass, as well as why you should be consuming it. You can also find a variety of products to purchase on the site.

You can also see some great videos here:

Learn to grow wheatgrass:
http://www.youtube.com/watch?v=gS8Xch0G0jM

Or at this site: http://www.howcast.com/videos/217950-How-to-Grow-Wheatgrass

To purchase juicers, consider the options listed at:

- Amazon.com

- WheatGrassKits.com

To purchase wheatgrass seeds, consider the following suppliers, though it is up to you to ensure the product you buy is organic and of utmost quality too!

Amazon.com has a variety of retailers. Be sure to learn as much as you can about the product you are buying before you decide to invest in it. Some retailers even have their product fulfilled by Amazon so it is eligible for Amazon Prime's free 2-day shipping.

Wheatgrasskits.com sells not only a variety of seed options but also kits to help you to grow them easily. This site has some organic options that are worth investing in because they have the USDA Organic label and are non-GMO options.

For more recipes, check out these options:

http://www.wheatgrass.com/t-wheat-grass-recipes.aspx

SproutPeople.org also has a section on wheatgrass

Most importantly, keep exploring the many ways to use and benefit from wheatgrass. You may just want to try different options or even just enjoy it in its raw, unjuiced state. No matter what you do, you'll find that this is one nutrition your body loves to have.

More by Julia Winchester

If you enjoyed this book, you might consider checking out my first book, Microgreens: A Beginner's Guide to the Benefits of Cultivation and Consumption.

It is available as both a paperback and Kindle version through Amazon.com.